Rocks & Plants

For the kids close by: Andrew and Allie,
who inspired us from the start, Mark, Kelsey,
Henning and Anna, for your love, encouragement
and fine outlook on life! With love.
—M.C. & C.C.

I dedicate this book to God and
to my son Elijah. Son, may you grow
up in God's light and follow his will.
—T.K.

GOD's Creation SERIES

Rocks & Plants

Written & Illustrated by

Michael & Caroline Carroll

Cartoons by Travis King

zonderkidz

www.zonderkidz.com

Book 3: Rocks & Plants
Text and illustration copyright © 2005 by Michael and Caroline Carroll
Cartoons copyright © 2005 Travis King
Photo on page 8: Sigurdur Thorarinsson
Photo on page 12: NASA
Top photo on page 15: Ray Fleshman, courtest Mount Saint Helens Creation Information Center.
Photo on pages 21 & 31: Bill Gerrish
Photo on page 23: Dale Andersen, USGS

Requests for information should be addressed to:
Zonderkidz, Grand Rapids, Michigan 49530

Library of Congress Cataloging-in-Publication Data

Carroll, Michael W., 1955-
  Rocks & plants / written and illustrated by Michael and Caroline Carroll ; cartoons by Travis King.- 1st ed.
     p. cm. – (God's creation series ; bk. 3)
  ISBN 0-310-70580-0 (softcover)
  1. Creation–Juvenile literature. 2. Nature–Religious aspects–Christianity–Juvenile literature.
[1. Creation. 2. Nature–Religious aspects–Christianity.] I. Title: Rocks and plants. II. Carroll,
Caroline, 1956- III. King, Travis ill. IV. Title.
  BS651.C3347 2005
  231.7'65–dc22

                                                                        2003026700

Editor: Barbara Scott
Art direction & design: Laura Maitner-Mason
Production artist: Sarah Jongsma
Cover design: Chris Tobias
Scientific review, rocks: Dr. Stephen O. Moshier, Wheaton College
Scientific review, plants: Dr. Corinne Carlson
Theological review: Dr. Stanley R. Allaby

Printed in China
05 06 07 08 09/CTC/5 4 3 2 1

A Special Word About

God's Creation Series

God created the heavens and the earth, and lots of other cool stuff too! We divided our books up in a way that is like the creation week described in Genesis, but we put a few things in different places so that we can understand them better. In Book One we talk about the beginning of the universe along with the stars and planets, while the Bible talks about the sun, moon, and stars on the fourth day. Don't worry—we noticed! God's Creation Series is about the wonders of God's creation, and not so much about when each event took place. So hold on for the ride of your life—through time and space—to enjoy the great things made by our great God!

God said,"Let the water under the sky be gathered to one place and let dry ground appear." And it was so. God called the dry ground "land," and the gathered waters he called "seas." And God saw that it was good.

Genesis 1:9-10

Layers in glacier ice leave a record of the past.

On the second day, God separated the waters above from the waters below. Clouds appeared in the sky and oceans formed, but there was no dry land. The earth was still hot from the energy of creation, but soon the rock of the earth began to cool, and the continents rose from the sea. Within these continents—where you and all your friends live—we find a beautiful record of what has come before. Layers in the rocks, lines in coral reefs, deposits in glaciers, and rings in trees show that God has written the history of creation for us in the Bible and in the earth.

Surtsey

What was it like when God brought forth the first land from the seas? The world got a glimpse of that strange time when the island of Surtsey was born. Surtsey is off the coast of Iceland, but it hasn't been there for long. In November 1963, there was nothing but ocean sloshing around Iceland's shores. Suddenly, on November 17—*ka-blooey!*—a column of steam and ash blasted from the sea. The water boiled and hot stones shot two miles up into the sky! A cone of lava and ash rose out of the water. The ocean waves constantly beat it back, but new eruptions built the tiny island up again. Soon, Surtsey displayed two volcanic craters, with gray sand dunes in between and a necklace of glowing lava around its edge. What a sight that must have been! Over the next four years, eruptions built Surtsey into a permanent island.

The smoke billowed up from it like smoke from a furnace, and the whole mountain trembled violently.

Exodus 19:18

Shortly after Surtsey settled down, the first life arrived. It was a sea rocket plant. This scene was a rerun of one that played out over and over during the early days of creation. God had caused the land to form and then prepared it to sustain the plants and grasses, seeds and trees that would come later. Now it's time to explore how the rocks, sand, soil, mountains, and valleys got here.

What we know for sure is that this time, it rained so much the whole earth was covered in water. Not only did rain fall from the sky, but it came from inside the earth through volcanoes. It still does today!

The Gospel in the Rocks

Many places in the Bible tell us that God shows himself through his creation (Romans 1:20, Psalm 19:1-4, Job 12:7). God has written a magnificent story beneath your feet. The layers of rock tell of huge floods, thundering volcanoes, and a rich parade of living things in many forms.

The rocks describe these great events, some of which are mentioned in the Bible. Many Christians have studied the rocks, too. Almost two hundred years ago, and English pastor named William Buckland became fascinated with the

William Buckland

As you read this, there are 600 active volcanoes rumbling and gushing all over the world.

More than a thousand years ago, Vikings saw volcanic eruptions in the ocean.

collection of dinosaur footprints.

Hitchcock taught his students how to be missionaries and take the gospel to far-away lands. He encouraged them to bring back rocks from the places they visited. Hitchcock often included geology into his sermons, telling his congregation that God's truth could be seen displayed in the Bible and in the world around them. He believed that the history of the world unfolded over time, and that God created in steps, just as Genesis says it did.

Edward Hitchcock

connection between the Bible and geology (the study of rocks). He spent much of his time trying to understand how the two work together. Buckland often went through the English countryside looking for interesting rocks. Buckland's horse was so used to stopping at interesting rock outcrops that when Buckland fell asleep during long rides, the horse would stop at large stones and wake up his rider! Buckland was also the first person to describe a dinosaur, which he called "The Great Fossil Lizard of Stonesfield."

Reverend Edward Hitchcock was also a student of the history found in the earth's rocks. In addition to being a pastor and the first state geologist of Massachusetts, Hitchcock created the world's largest

Both Hitchcock and Buckland realized that the awesome power and splendor of God is echoed in the earth's fossils, stones, and mountains. They both saw the same message in the rocks: a loving creator—one interested in details—sculpted the earth.

Fitting the Pieces Together

Just like a cosmic loaf of bread, the earth's outer layer is called the crust. But the crust is not one solid chunk. It's broken into pieces that fit loosely together. These pieces

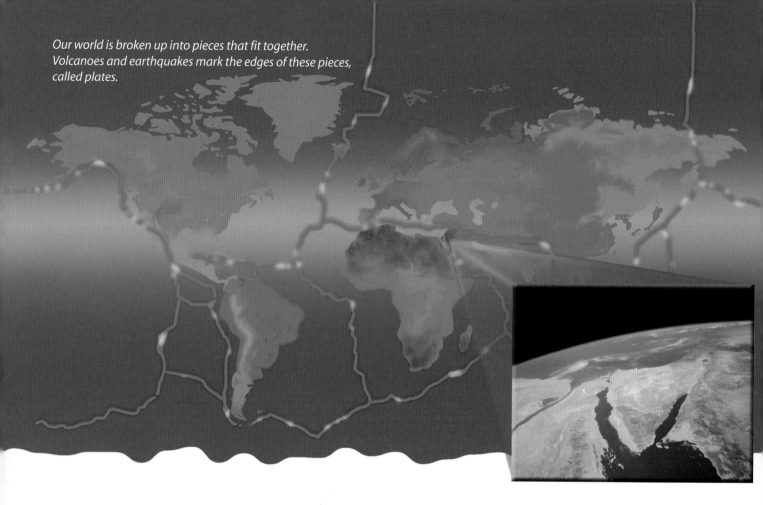

Our world is broken up into pieces that fit together. Volcanoes and earthquakes mark the edges of these pieces, called plates.

are called plates. The plates float on a sea of molten (melted) rock. The movement of these plates is called plate tectonics. It's God's conveyor belt!

Some plates grind against each other, which causes earthquakes. Some plates have shoved each other up, folding rocky layers and pushing up mountains. In other places, one plate dives underneath another and melts away deep inside the earth.

In the middle of the Atlantic Ocean, there is a "rift zone," or place where two plates meet. The rift zone makes new plate material that moves toward the continents. On the other side of the

world, at the mid-Pacific ridge, plates slide under one another. They move in many other directions across the world, too.

At this place in Iceland, the plates of the Atlantic rift zone can be seen moving apart as the valley of Thingvellir spreads with newly made rock.

The Geologic Column

A geologic column is like a layer cake made of stone. It's a series of rock layers that show how the ground was put together in that place. Usually the most recent rock layer is at the top (makes sense, right?), although sometimes plate tectonics have turned the layers sideways or upside down.

All over the earth, columns of rock can be found in orders that match up with others in different places. When you compare them, you can easily see how God put the world together in a certain order.

Good examples of shifted layers can be found in mountain areas, where the sequence of rocks has been folded over upon itself. For example, let's say we find layer A on top, then B, C, and D with E at the very bottom. The layer sequence next to the mountains may be EDCBABCDE. Can you figure out what happened here? To make things even more confusing, sometimes the top of the mountain has been washed away, so we might find EDCBABC. But you never find shuffled, mixed up layers (ADBCEAC).

The geologic column is made of many layers from lakeshores, volcanic ash, flood sediments, and even ocean floor dirt.

13

Reading the Record

Some of the earliest fans of the geologic column idea were two Christian creationists: Adam Sedgwick and Roderick Murchison. They simply wrote down what they saw in the layers of the earth. Although the sequence of layers is often used when speaking about evolution, the theory of evolution came along long after the idea of the geologic column.

Certain kinds of fossils are found at each different layer. Dinosaur fossils are not found with elephants, and flamingos would not be found in deep, ancient layers with trilobites.

Big Floods

Floods have changed the face of our planet in many ways. Floods have carved great canyons and valleys. They are often triggered by volcanoes, which melt underground ice. Sometimes glaciers form a natural dam in a river, and when the glacier breaks, tons of water pours out (this happened across the middle of North America at the end of the last ice age, flooding the states of Washington and Idaho.) Floods often quickly bury animals and plants in mud, preserving them as fossils.

Water also works gradually over time. Some canyons are very old, having been carved out by rivers over countless centuries. The ocean pounds relentlessly at the rocks and beaches of the continents, changing the shoreline and keeping mapmakers busy.

The Bible relates the story of a great flood in Genesis 6:14. God tells Noah to build an ark to save his family and the animals that populated the earth. A story of a great flood is also told in ancient Babylonian writings.

CAN YOU FIND THE GEOLOGIC COLUMN IN THE WALLS OF THE GRAND CANYON?

Three pieces of a puzzle

Look at the layers in these rocks! How did they form?

Top photo: The flat layers in the top photo were put down in less than twenty-four hours after Mount St. Helens erupted and caused mudslides. Most rock layers do not form this fast.

Middle photo: The layers at the foot of the Rocky Mountains, which are made of sand and mud, are very thick and are only part of thousands of layers in the mountain ranges. When they formed, they were flat, like at Mount St. Helens, but not caused by volcanic mudslides or one big flood. When the mountains formed, the layers were pushed up and tilted.

Bottom photo: Water cannot fold layers like the ones shown here. When tectonic plates move against each other, the rock layers break and fold like crumpled-up paper.

Around and Around

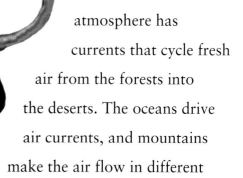

The world is like a chili pepper—cool on the outside but hot on the inside.

Much of our world's energy is stored at the core of our planet. But to understand the wonders of Earth's guts, we must understand that the earth is the ultimate recycling factory.

We find cycles in water, air, and even in the rocks! As we saw on the second day, the atmosphere has currents that cycle fresh air from the forests into the deserts. The oceans drive air currents, and mountains make the air flow in different directions.

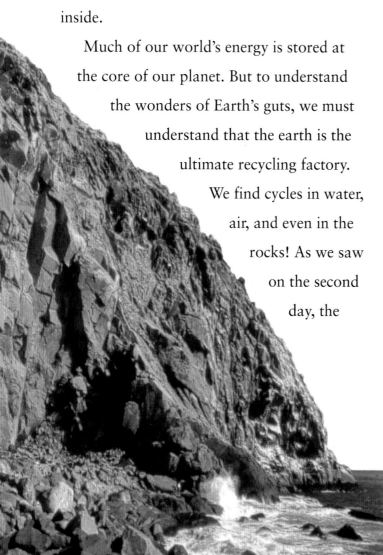

Remember the water cycle from Book Two? Water rains down and runs into the ocean, where it evaporates and forms clouds to rain another day. This big wet Ferris wheel is part of God's intricate design, bringing minerals from the high mountains down to the plains and onto the ocean floor. If the earth relied solely on the water cycle, all the good minerals that plants and people need would end up at the bottom of the sea. But God has given Earth another built-in recycling machine to take care of that.

At the water's edge, a complex dance of chemistry and erosion takes place. This is how it works. Rain and wind break down the mountains. Rocks, gravel, and sand wash down the slopes into valleys and plains. Eventually, all this mountain stuff ends up in the ocean.

So why do we even have mountains? Remember those plate tectonics? When the world's plates are shoved under each other, the rocks and minerals from the mountains melt. This melted rock rises back to the top when other plates shove each other up as new mountain ranges, or when a volcano builds another, just like Surtsey. Continents shift and mountains rise. In this way, rocks are recycled like rain and air.

THE EARTH'S CORE IS STILL BOILING HOT. WHAT'S UP WITH THAT?

In the beginning, the earth was a big ball of hot rock that began cooling off as soon as God made it. But why is it still hot? Some say it's because the earth hasn't been around very long. But there are other reasons that might explain why the earth is still hot. Let's take a look at some of the clues God has left us.

Way back in 1897, a scientist named Lord Kelvin guessed that when the world was created, it was hot, liquid rock. He figured out that if the earth continued cooling from that day on, then it was about twenty-five million years old. But the earth doesn't cool that way. The inside of the earth is also heated by radioactive rocks. These rocks cool off much more slowly than lava.

This can be seen in other planets, too! So even though the leftover heat of creation would be long gone, if the earth were very old, there is still heat from radioactive rocks like uranium. The earth's temperature does not doesn't prove that the world is young or old.

As with many things, the story is more rich and complex than that, and a little harder to figure out. But that's okay, part of the fun of science is trying to figure it all out and knowing that only God has all the answers.

SO THAT'S HOW GOD DID IT!

Lava in the Back Yard

One sunny day on the island of Hawaii, the jungle mountainside is calm and peaceful. Suddenly, the mountain rumbles. Ash begins to spew from the peak, and a terrible, sulphur smell fills the air. Nearby residents throw children, pets, and a few belongings into their cars and speed away. Now, at the mountaintop an orange glow appears, followed by billowing smoke. The jungle is on fire! Superheated lava, 2,000 degrees Fahrenheit, pours down from the the top of the volcano, burning everything in its path. The lava pours down over a period of hours, slowing as it cools. Finally it reaches the narrow beach and the sea beyond. As the hot lava hits the cold water, steam billows hundreds of feet in the air.

Pahoehoe lava looks like twisted rope or taffy.

Weather Rocks!

The Rock Cycle is hard for us to see because it is *very* slow. If the water cycle is the hare, the rock cycle is the tortoise. Still, slow and steady wins the race. The rocks come and go just as the air and water do. In the water cycle, the heat from the sun drives air currents. Liquid water changes to vapor and rises into the sky to become clouds. Then it turns to liquid or ice as it falls to Earth as rain, hail, and snow.

Far beneath our feet, rock is being heated by the earth's core. It changes from one form to another as it rises, then falls back down again. As great slabs of granite (the rock which forms continents) slide under each other, they move downward, forty miles underground. The granite is crushed into a crystal "cloud" of rock minerals that only exist at very high temperatures and pressures. Eventually, the rock drifts apart and rises up again, like a stony rainstorm in reverse. At times, this super hot molten rock explodes up through the ground, erupting into the air as a volcano. Rock cycle meets air cycle!

Rock Concert

When rock comes out of the ground as lava it hardens into igneous rock. Wind, ice and rain break the rock down into gravel and sand. These bits of rock stick together in layers, becoming sedimentary rock. Some sedimentary rock, like limestone, is made of squished together plants or the shells of animals. As more stuff piles on top of the sedimentary rock, it changes into other forms of rock. Any rock that has changed is called metamorphic rock. For example, soft limestone becomes (or morphs) into hard marble.

Lepidolite

Beryl

Pyrite

Calcite

Epidote

Rose Quartz

Quartz

Smoky Quartz

Purpurite

Gypsum

Tourmaline

Microcline

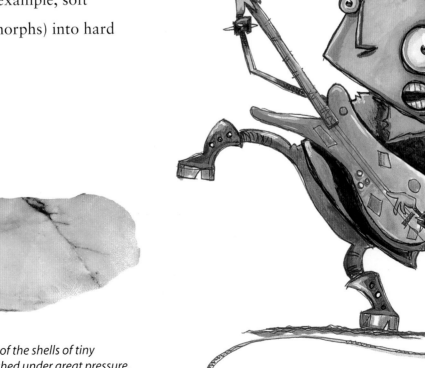

THESE ROCKS ROCK!

Limestone (on the left) is made of the shells of tiny animals. When limestone is crushed under great pressure, it turns hard and smooth, becoming marble (right).

Where Air and Rock Meet

An important part of the air's trip around Earth is called the carbon cycle. God has set this cycle in motion so that plants—and the rest of us—can live. Carbon is in lots of places, including the air. The air's carbon dioxide gas (CO_2) weighs as much as 760 billion cars!

HERE'S A SIMPLIFIED VERSION OF HOW THE CYCLES OF THE WORLD WORK TOGETHER.

Plants breathe in the CO_2. Animals and people eat the plants, and the carbon goes into them. Animals and people breathe out CO_2, and it's also released into the air as people, creatures, and plants die.

The ocean holds twenty times as much carbon as all the plants and animals on earth, and fifty times as much as the air. Rocks, too, have carbon, and they have the most, more than fifty thousand times the amount the atmosphere has. Because of the rock cycle, carbon slowly sinks into the rocks and then is put back into the air through volcanoes and geysers.

AIR CYCLE

CARBON CYCLE

WEATHER

ROCK CYCLE

EROSION

WATER CYCLE

The ocean's carbon is soaking into these rocks.
Where will it go next?

The Plants: God's Leafy Masterpieces

When the cycles of the earth were in place, the stage was set for the first kind of life that God created—plants! He created them in every imaginable size, shape, and color. He put them in the deepest oceans, the driest deserts, and even in the hottest volcanoes.

So far, about 350 *thousand* species of plants have been discovered. Genesis 1:11-12 tells us what happened on the third day:

Then God said, "Let the land produce vegetation: seed-bearing plants and trees on the land that bear fruit with seeds in it, according to their various kinds." And it was so. The land produced vegetation: plants bearing seed according to their kinds...And God saw that it was good.

But in Genesis 1:14-19—on the fourth day—we read,

And God said, "Let there be lights in the expanse of the sky to separate the day from the night..."

Critics of the Bible point out that God created plants on the third day, before the sun appeared on the fourth day. But plants need light to grow, so what happened?

> Who cuts a channel for the torrents of rain, and a path for the thunderstorm, to water a land where no man lives, a desert with no one in it?
>
> Job 38: 25–26

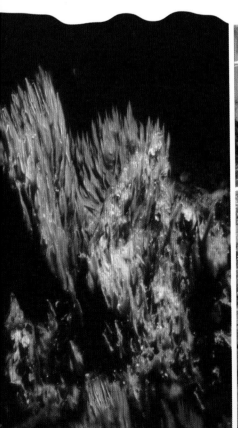

Plants live at the bottom of the ocean (left), on mountains (center) and even in volcanoes (right)!

A solar-power factory built by people, and some solar-power factories created by God. Which works better?

- People wear plants (cotton and linen).

- People drink plants (tea, coffee, juice, Coca-Cola).

- People eat plants (all those salad leaves, mushrooms, nuts, beans, fruits, and vegetables).

- People sit and sleep on plants (furniture).

- People get most of their medicines from plants.

- People put plants in their gas tanks (gasoline is made from petroleum, which includes ancient plants).

The Genesis story of creation seems to be told from the viewpoint of someone living on the earth's surface. Scientists who study the history of planets say that Earth's air was probably cloudy at first. From the ground, a person whould not be able to see the sun, moon, and stars, yet sunlight would still be able to get through. As plants breathed out oxygen, God may have used the plans to clear out air. If so, the things in the sky would be visible on the fourth day. In this way, science seems to be saying the same thing God's word says.

How Plants Work

God designed plants to use sunlight for energy. They are the only things God created that can make their own

food. Inside each plant leaf is a tiny little factory. This factory takes in sunlight, adds water and carbon dioxide, and turns these raw materials into its own food, in the form of sugar. Then, like all factories, it puts out its waste products— water and oxygen. This process is called photosynthesis.

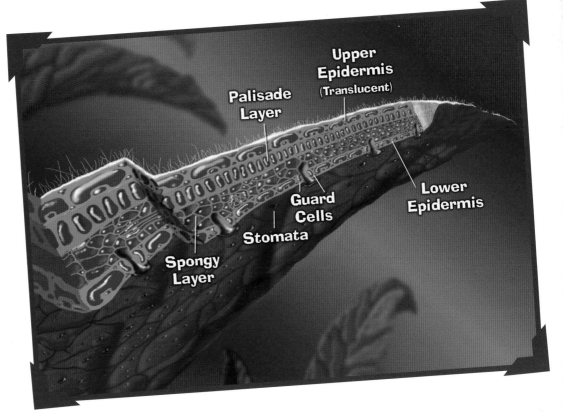

Upper Epidermis (Translucent)

Palisade Layer

Lower Epidermis

Guard Cells

Stomata

Spongy Layer

Fun Facts

The biggest flower in the world is the orange and white *Rafflesia arnoldi*, which blooms in the jungles of Southeast Asia. It can weigh up to fifteen pounds and be three feet wide. It also smells like rotting meat, to attract insects. Yummy!

The floating duckweed is the smallest flowering plant in the world. The entire plant measures less than one twenty-fifth of an inch, and its fruit is smaller than a grain of salt.

Changing Colors

When fall comes to places with warm summers and cold winters, the leaves change with the weather. The plant or tree gets ready to take a nap—kind of like a hibernating animal. It doesn't need to make food anymore, so it doesn't need chlorophyll. The green chlorophyll dies out,

leaving the other colors that were always there, hidden by the green: red, yellow, or orange. The leaves dry and fall off, making room for new green leaves next spring.

Flowering Plants

About two-thirds of all the plants in the world make flowers. Flowers contain pollen. The pollen is spread to other plants of the same kind by wind or insects attracted to the bright, yummy-smelling flowers. After the pollen meets with pollen from another plant, the flowers make seeds. That's how some plants make new plants. The seeds drop to the ground or get blown by the wind to a new place to grow. Coconut trees drop their seeds—coconuts—on the beach, and they float away to other islands to grow.

Coconuts are the biggest seeds in the world.

There's a Fungus Among Us!

They look like they're out of a cheap science fiction movie, but these weird plants are awesome. Mushrooms and molds are not exactly plants, because they can grow in the dark and can't make their own food from sunlight. They get their food from dead or living plants and animals. They put out spores (tiny particles as fine as baby powder) instead of seeds to grow more fungi.

Plants That Bite Back

Venus flytraps, pitcher plants, and sundews all eat bugs and sometimes frogs or fish. Tasty! About five hundred species of carnivorous (meat-eating) plants have been discovered so far. The best-known carnivorous plant is the Venus flytrap. Its leaves are split open with spines on the edges. When an insect lands on the leaf, the two sides of the leaf snap together, and then the leaf slowly digests its meal.

SNAP!

The Australian sundew plant has sticky leaves two feet long. When an unwary frog lands on a leaf, he gets stuck to it. Then the leaf rolls up around the frog and digests him. Pitcher plants have tunnels leading to "pitchers" of nectar. Once an insect crawls into the tunnel, a one-way trap door prevents him from getting out. Dinner is served!

COULD YOU DESIGN FIFTY THOUSAND KINDS OF TREES? BOY, I COULDN'T. GOD SURE IS AMAZING!

Trees

Trees are the giants of the plant family. A tree is a plant with a long, woody stem called a trunk. Each tree has roots, leaves, and a trunk covered with bark. Some trees have pinecones and some have flowers. Some have leaves, and some have needles, which are really just long, skinny leaves. The leaves of a cactus are its spines. There are more than fifty thousand kinds of trees. Every kind has its own shape and leaf.

Tree Rings

The trunk of a tree grows a new ring each year of its life. Like candles on a birthday cake, counting the rings will tell you the age of the tree. Scientists can also study the rings to learn which years were extra dry or cold, and sometimes they can even learn when there was a forest fire. They have a spiffy way of studying the rings without cutting the tree down. They use a special tool to cut a "core sample" out of the tree to see the ring history without killing the tree.

The Gift of Trees

Trees are a wonderful blessing. They provide homes for many kinds of animals, as well as water, oxygen, and shade. The wood from trees can be used to make paper, pencils, lumber for homes and other buildings, cardboard boxes, furniture, violins, and cuckoo clocks. Wood can also be burned for heat and energy. Fruit and nuts come from trees and also the maple tree sap to make maple syrup, which you can pour on your pancakes.

The root system of a tree is hidden, but it's often even bigger than the leafy part of the tree.

The roots of a giant sequoia tree may stretch for three acres underground! God designed them to do many things. The roots hold the tree up and keep it from blowing over. They bring in groundwater and minerals for the tree to use to make food, and hold the soil around the tree in place, so it can't wash away in the rain or blow away in the wind.

LIKE SNOWFLAKES, NO TWO LEAVES ON A TREE ARE EXACTLY ALIKE.

Fun Facts

The *tallest* tree in the world is a coast redwood 368 feet tall. It's called "Mendocino Tree," and is in Montgomery State Reserve in California.

The *oldest* tree in the world is "Methuselah," a bristle-cone pine in the White Mountains of California that's over 4,700 years old. It was a seedling when the first cities were being built in Mesopotamia at the time of Abraham!

Plants That Feed Us

Plants are the first link in the food chain. One way or another, all other living things rely on plants for food. People are the last link in the food chain, because they eat foods that come straight from plants, such as fruits and vegetables, juices and teas, beans and nuts, breads, cereals and grains, and spices.

But people also eat food from animals. In a sense, they are still eating plants, though, because the meat comes from animals that ate plants. Cows, for example, eat grass. People drink cow's milk, eat cheese and yogurt, and pig out on hamburgers. They eat eggs and the chickens that lay them. People eat fish, lobsters, crabs, and insects, all of which rely on plants or other animals for food.

Plants That Heal

God filled the world with plants that could be used to heal sickness and disease. It would take a whole book to list all the plants that heal, but here are a few examples:

- The juice of the aloe vera stops the pain of burns.
- Garlic lowers high cholesterol and blood pressure, and helps cure colds.
- Willow bark helps pain and fevers; scientists copied its chemistry to make aspirin.
- The opium poppy is used to make morphine and codeine, which help severe pain.

From the Deepest Oceans to the Highest Peaks

The ocean is full of plant life, from tiny one-celled diatoms to giant kelp—the fastest growing plant in the world. Kelp can grow up to twelve inches per day!

The Himalayas in Asia are the tallest mountains in the world. But even there, at twenty thousand feet, flowering plants grow in the shelter of rocks. If you are ever up in the mountains above the tree line, look at the small plants at your feet. They hug the ground and grow in mats so the wind doesn't blow them away.

Arctic plants stay low to the ground.

Scripture Cake

Try this fun recipe for making a cake using ingredients from Bible verses. It is called Scripture Cake, and it's delicious.

1 ¹/₂ cups Judges 5:25
3 cups Jeremiah 6:20
6 Isaiah 10:14
3 ¹/₂ cups 1 Kings 4:22
2 tsp Amos 4:5
a pinch of Matthew 5:13
several tsp. of 2 Chronicles 9:9
1 cup Genesis 24:17
2 tbsp Proverbs 24:13
2 cups dried Nahum 3:12
2 cups 1 Samuel 30:12
2 cups slivered or chopped
    Numbers 17:8

Cream together butter and sugar, and then beat in the eggs. Sift flour, baking powder, and spices together. Add, alternating with water, to butter mixture. Add honey, figs, raisins, and almonds. Mix well. Put into two well-greased 9x5 loaf pans. Bake at 350 degrees for one hour.

Taking Care of God's Garden

Each year, many plants become extinct. In the United States alone, more than 3,000 kinds of plants are in danger of dying out. God calls on us to take care of the world he has given us, and that includes his forests, jungles, and wetlands.

The trees, plants, flowers, and mosses all take part in the song of the world—a song which tells the joyful story of a God who creates in beauty and balance. The book of Isaiah says: *The mountains and hills will burst into song before you, and all the trees of the field will clap their hands.*—Isaiah 55:12

At the end of the third creation day, after the plants had taken hold, God's new world was ready for the first creatures. They would arrive on the fourth day.

The world is so full of a number of things, I'm sure we should all be as happy as kings.
—Robert Louis Stevenson

One day, Jesus' disciples were praising God for the miracles they had seen. Someone told Jesus that he should make his disciples be quiet, but Jesus said, "If they keep quiet, even the stones will cry out." The stones of the mountains, the sands of the beaches, the granite peaks, thundering volcanoes, rocky cliffs, and winding valleys all cry out to the majesty of their maker.

Index

GOD's Creation SERIES

BOOK 1

Space & Time

zonderkidz

Written & Illustrated by Michael & Caroline Carroll
Cartoons by Travis King

LIKE SNOWFLAKES, NO TWO LEAVES ON A TREE ARE EXACTLY ALIKE.

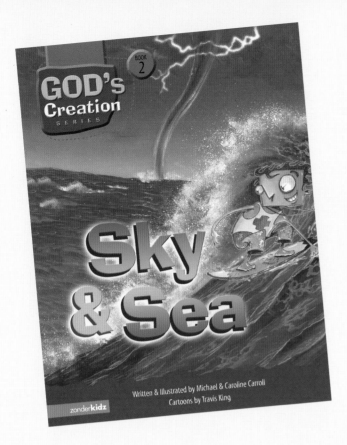

God's Creation Series

Written & Illustrated by Michael and Caroline Carroll

Cartoons by Travis King

Kids will enjoy learning about creation with this set of books—for ages 6 & up

Cartoons, artistic renderings, photographs, fun facts, and more make these informative and entertaining books on creation a rich visual experience— while presenting scientific information.

Space & Time
Book 1
ISBN: 0-310-70578-9

Rocks & Plants
Book 3
ISBN: 0-310-70580-0

Sky & Sea
Book 2
ISBN: 0-310-70579-7

Fish, Bugs & Birds
Book 4
ISBN: 0-310-70581-9